The Best Butter

Book!

Fantastic Flavors of Homemade Butters,

Spreads & Sauces

BY

Christina Tosch

Copyright Notes

Table of Contents

Introduction

It was only a few years ago that due to its high saturated fat content, butter was given the thumbs down.

Today though, with more people turning their backs on low-fat diets, which can lead to consuming more carbs and sugars, butter is back!

Not all fats are bad; it's a fact. Eaten in moderation, some dairy products, including butter, have been linked to a reduced risk of diabetes, heart problems, and obesity.

This vitamin rich product is well and truly making a return to family mealtimes.

Whether you use it as a topping for toast, for melting on meats, or as an ingredient for buttery spreads and sauces, you can't beat the taste of flavored or homemade butter.

Do you want to make homemade butter from scratch? Would you like to give the butter a boost with sweet and savory flavorings, create sensational homemade butter sauces, or experiment with dairy-free homemade butter recipes? Then look no further than the Best Butter Book!

Nothing tastes better than these 40 fantastic flavors of homemade butters, spreads & sauces!

Nut, Seed & Dairy-Free Butters

California Walnut Butter

This butter makes a great dip and is fantastic with fresh fruit. It's easy to make and is super-handy to have in the fridge.

Servings: 1 (14 ounce) jar

Total Time: 5mins

Ingredients:

- 2 cups Californian raw walnuts
- ¼ tsp salt
- 2 tsp vegetable oil
- Honey (to taste, optional)

Directions:

1. Add the raw walnuts to a food processor and grind to a paste-like consistency.
2. Add the salt and the oil, a little at a time, and process until the butter binds together.
3. Taste and sweeten with honey if needed.
4. Transfer to a resealable glass jar and store in the fridge.

Cashew Butter

This mild-tasting butter is a great substitute for any recipes that ask for cream or milk. It works as well in soups and sauces as it does for shakes and cheesecake desserts.

Servings: 1 (16 ounce) jar

Total Time: 35mins

Ingredients:

- 4 cups raw cashews
- 2 tsp extra-virgin coconut oil

Directions:

1. Preheat the main oven to 325 degrees.
2. Scatter the cashews in a single layer on a baking sheet and toast in the oven until golden brown. This will take 10-15 minutes.
3. Allow the nuts to cool on the pan for 8-10 minutes.
4. Add the cooled cashew nuts to a food processor and process for approximately 10 minutes until a slightly creamy consistency. Scrape down the sides of the processor bowl as needed.
5. While the processor motor is running, add the coconut oil and process for an additional 5 minutes, until the butter is our preferred consistency.
6. Spoon the butter into a resealable glass container and store in the refrigerator.

Coconut Butter

Use this smooth and creamy butter straight from the jar, put it over porridge, add it to your morning smoothie or spread it over toast. There really is nothing better than this dairy-free butter.

Servings: 1 (16 ounce) jar

Total Time: 24hours 15mins

Ingredients:

- 6 cups unsweetened shredded coconut
- ½ cup coconut oil
- ¼ tsp Himalayan salt

Directions:

1. Add the shredded coconut, coconut oil, and salt to a food processor and process until a creamy liquid; this will take 8-10 minutes. Scrape down the sides of the bowl as needed.
2. Force the mixture through a fine-mesh sieve while pushing it down using a rubber spatula or ladle.
3. Return the butter that remains in the sieve to the processor and process once more for 2-3 minutes until it is a liquid once again.
4. Once again, force the mixture through the fine-mesh sieve. You may need to repeat this process 1-2 times more to make the most of your coconut.
5. Pour the smooth butter into a 16-ounce glass, resealable jar, and allow it to sit, undisturbed for a minimum of 24 hours.
6. Use as needed.

Hazelnut Butter

Drizzle this butter over French toast, waffles, yogurt, oatmeal, or fresh fruit, and enjoy this nutritious and nutty butter.

Servings: 2 (14 ounce) jars

Total Time: 30mins

Ingredients:

- 1 pound raw hazelnuts
- ½-1 tsp ground cinnamon
- ½ tsp sea salt

- 2-3 tsp coconut sugar

Directions:

1. Preheat the main oven to 350 degrees F.
2. Arrange the hazelnuts in a single layer to a roasting tray. Roast the nuts in the oven until fragrant and golden, this will take 12-15 minutes.
3. Remove the nuts from the oven and allow to slightly cool before transferring to a kitchen towel. Using your hands, roll the hazelnuts around and remove the skins.
4. Add the raw hazelnuts, minus the skins, to a high-speed food blender or processor, and on low, blend to create a smooth butter, for 7-9 minutes. You will need to scrape down the sides of the bowl as necessary.
5. Once the butter is smooth and creamy, add the cinnamon, sea salt, and coconut sugar.
6. On puree, blend until combined. Taste and adjust the seasonings.
7. Transfer the butter to 2 (14 ounce) jars and store for up to 21 days at room temperature or in the fridge for up to 8 weeks.

Peanut Butter

Forget store-bought peanut butter and instead make your own with the comfort of knowing there are no added sweeteners or nasty additives.

Servings: 1 (12 ounce) jar

Total Time: 10mins

Ingredients:

- 2 cups dry-roasted peanuts
- 1–2 tbsp honey
- Sea salt (to taste)

Directions:

1. Add the peanuts to a food processor and process for 4-5 minutes until a creamy smooth liquid.
2. Stir in the honey and add salt to taste, if necessary.
3. Transfer to a resealable glass jar and store in the fridge for up to 6 weeks.

Pecan Butter

Wake-up to a breakfast that includes homemade pecan butter, add it to oatmeal, blend it into smoothies or spread it on toast.

Servings: 1 (12 ounce) jar

Total Time: 10mins

Ingredients:

- Nonstick cooking spray
- 12 ounces raw pecans (coarsely chopped)
- Pinch of salt
- ½ tsp cinnamon
- 1 tbsp brown sugar

Directions:

1. Preheat the main oven to 350 degrees F.
2. Spray a cookie sheet with nonstick cooking spray.
3. Arrange the pecans on the cookie sheet in a single layer and toast until fragrant, for 5 minutes. Set aside to cool.
4. Once the pecans are sufficiently cool, transfer to a high-speed food blender along with a pinch of salt, cinnamon, and brown sugar.
5. On moderate to moderate-high speed, process for 50 seconds until you achieve your preferred consistency. You may need to stir the butter a few times. Taste and adjust the seasoning, adding more salt or sugar, as needed.
6. Transfer the butter to a resealable glass container and allow to completely cool before placing in the refrigerator.

Pistachio Butter

This butter is one of the easiest and healthiest butters to make at home. It's a versatile spread for savory crepes and sweet pancakes or as a flavoring for mousse, ice cream and buttercream.

Servings: 1 (12 ounce) jar

Total Time: 6mins

Ingredients:

- 1 cup butter (softened)
- ¼ cup organic honey
- 1 tbsp apricot gelatin powder
- ¼ cup pistachios (chopped)

Directions:

1. In a small-size mixing bowl, beat the butter along with the honey and apricot gelatin powder until silky smooth. Stir in pistachios to combine.
2. Transfer to a glass airtight containers and store in the refrigerator for up to 28 days.
3. Use as needed.

Pumpkin Seed Butter

This pumpkin butter is sweet and spicy and can be used as a viable alternative to peanut butter. It is the perfect pairing with lots of different snacks.

Servings: 1 (8 ounce) jar

Total Time: 25mins

Ingredients:

- 1 cup whole almonds
- 1½ cups pumpkin seeds (shelled)
- 1 tbsp maple syrup
- ¼ cup canola oil
- ¼ tsp cumin
- ¼ tsp ginger
- ¼ tsp cinnamon

Directions:

1. Add the almonds, pumpkin seeds, maple syrup, canola oil, cumin, ginger, and cinnamon to a high-powdered food processor or food blender.
2. Process the mixture to a crunchy consistency and then to a smooth paste.
3. Transfer to a glass resealable jar and store in the fridge.

Roasted Almond Butter

This intense nut butter works well with sweet and savory recipes. It's also great in smoothies or to serve as a snack with dates.

Servings: 2 (10 ounce) jars

Total Time: 30mins

Ingredients:

- 4 cups raw almonds

Directions:

1. Preheat the main oven to 355 degrees f.
2. Add 2 cups of the almonds to a baking dish and roast for approximately 10 minutes, until golden. Remove from the oven and completely cool.
3. Place the almonds to a food processor and blend to a creamy paste, this will take 5-10 minutes.
4. Store in a resealable glass container and store at room temperature for up to 3 months.

Sesame Seed Butter

Homemade tahini or sesame seed butter is ideal for making hummus, spreading on toast, stirring into soup, or using as a salad dressing.

Servings: 1 (6-8 ounce) jar*

Total Time: 8mins

Ingredients:

- 1 cup hulled sesame seeds
- 3 tbsp extra-virgin olive oil

Directions:

1. Over moderate-high heat, heat a clean and dry heavy skillet, and add the sesame seeds. Cook while frequently stirring until golden. Once golden, continually stir while taking care not to burn the seeds.
2. Once toasted, allow to cool for a few minutes before adding to a food processor.
3. Begin by adding 3 tablespoons of olive oil to the processor and process the mixture into a paste consistency. You may need to add more olive oil. Scrape down the sides of the bowl as needed.
4. Stir the butter well and transfer to a resealable glass jar in the refrigerator for up to 6 months.

*The amount of butter depends on the quantities of olive oil used

Soy Butter

Soy butter is better than peanut butter! It has great taste and texture but is cholesterol-free and contains less saturated fat making it a great choice for anyone watching their weight.

Servings: 1 (8 ounce) jar

Total Time: 35mins

Ingredients:

- ½ cup unsoaked organic soybeans
- 2 tbsp grapeseed oil
- ⅛ tsp salt
- ¼ cup water

Directions:

1. Preheat the main oven to 350 degrees F.
2. Add the soybeans to a colander and rinse under cold running water.
3. Transfer the soybeans onto a plate lined with a kitchen paper towel and briefly pat dry.
4. Arrange the soybeans on a cookie sheet. Drizzle over 1 tablespoon of oil and mix to coat the soybeans evenly.
5. Transfer the cookie sheet to the middle rack of the preheated oven and roast until golden, for 20 minutes.
6. Remove from the oven and allow to cool for 5 minutes, at room temperature.
7. Transfer the roasted beans to a high-speed blender and process until smooth.
8. Spoon the butter into a resealable glass jar and place in the fridge for up to 10 days.

Sunflower Seed Butter

Sunflower has a tendency to be a little bitter-tasting, but the added extras of coconut sugar, coconut oil, and cinnamon will help to combat this. This butter tastes so good you will be able to eat it straight from the jar.

Servings: 1 (14 ounce) jar

Total Time: 12mins

Ingredients:

- 3 cups raw shelled sunflower seeds
- ¼ cup coconut sugar
- 2 tbsp virgin coconut oil (softened)
- Pinch of pink Himalaya salt
- ½ tsp cinnamon
- 1 tsp pure vanilla essence
- 1 vanilla bean (seeded)

Directions:

1. Preheat the main oven to 325 degrees. Using parchment paper, line a baking sheet. Roast in the oven for 8-12 minutes, until some of the sunflower seeds are lightly golden. Allow to cool for 3-4 minutes before progressing on with the recipe.
2. In the meantime, add the coconut sugar to a high-speed food blender and grind until powder consistency. Set aside with the lid on, to allow the ground dust to settle.

3. Transfer the toasted sunflower seeds to a food processor and process for 3 minutes, while scraping down the processor bowl every 60 seconds. The mixture will be powder-like and dry at this stage.

4. Add the coconut oil to the food processor and process for another 2 minutes. The seed butter will clump into a large ball before it breaks down into a butter consistency. Again, scrape down the bowl as necessary.

5. Next, add the coconut sugar, Himalayan salt, and cinnamon. Process for another 2-3 minutes, until smooth.

6. Gradually and slowly stream in the vanilla essence while processing. Add the vanilla bean seeds. You may need to add a drop more coconut oil to thin out the consistency. Run the processor for a minimum of an additional 2 minutes until very smooth. This process will take 8-15 minutes, but the timings will depend on the type of processor.

7. Transfer the butter into a glass resealable container and chill in the fridge for up to 8 weeks.

Vegan Butter

Enjoy this healthy alternative to regular butter or margarine.

Servings: 1 (16 ounce) jar

Total Time: 5mins

Ingredients:

- ½ cup soy milk
- 2 tsp freshly squeezed lemon juice
- 1¼ cups coconut oil (melted)
- ¼ cup sunflower oil
- 2 tsp nutritional yeast
- ¾ tsp salt

Directions:

1. In a bowl, combine the milk with the lemon juice. Stir well and set aside to rest for 60-90 seconds; this will allow it to thicken and curdle.
2. Add the milk-lemon juice mixture followed by the coconut oil, sunflower oil, nutritional yeast, and salt to a food blender and process until smooth.
3. Pour the mixture into a resealable glass jar and transfer to the fridge, to set. You can store the butter in the fridge for up to 14-21 days.
4. When you are ready to serve, remove from the fridge to soften for 2-3 minutes.

Flavored Butters Spreads

Avocado Butter

Ripe avocado gives this butter a silky, smooth texture and fresh flavor, ideal for spreading over breakfast toast or crackers as an afternoon snack.

Servings: 8

Total Time: 5mins

Ingredients:

- ½ cup unsalted butter (at room temperature)
- 1 large ripe avocado (peeled, stoned)
- ½ tsp cumin
- 1½ tsp fresh lemon juice
- ½ tsp salt
- Black pepper

Directions:

1. Add the butter and avocado to a small food processor and blitz until silky smooth.
2. Add the cumin, lemon juice, salt, and a pinch of black pepper. Pulse until incorporated.
3. Enjoy the butter chilled or at room temperature.

Bacon-Bourbon Butter

Whip up a batch of this boozy butter and give grill meats or veggies a makeover. The crisp bacon bits hidden in the creamy butter add taste and texture to a juicy steak, too.

Servings: 8-12

Total Time: 25mins

Ingredients:

- 1 sliced smoked bacon (finely chopped)
- ½ cup unsalted butter (room temperature)
- 1 tbsp bourbon
- 1 tbsp pure maple syrup
- 1 tsp brown sugar
- Sea salt

Directions:

1. Over moderate heat, cook the bacon in a small-size frying pan, while occasionally stirring for 5-6 minutes, or until the bacon is crisp.

2. With a slotted spoon, transfer the crisp bacon to a plated lined with kitchen paper towel. Set 1 teaspoon of the bacon drippings to one side in a bowl.

3. To the bacon drippings, add the butter, bourbon, syrup, and sugar — season to taste with sea salt.

4. Using a metal fork, whisk the mixture vigorously until incorporated.

5. Crumble the crisp bacon and fold into the butter mixture until evenly combined.

6. Transfer the mixture to a piece of parchment paper. Place the mixture on the edge nearest to you. Fold the parchment paper over and roll into a log shape. Twist the ends to seal. Wrap the log in aluminum foil and chill in the fridge until sold.

7. You can store the butter in the fridge for up to 14 days or in the freezer for up to 12 weeks.

Basic Homemade Butter

Use this homemade butter just as you would any you buy in a store, for baking or straight from the butter dish.

Servings: 1 (10 ounce) jar

Total Time: 12mins

Ingredients:

- 3 cups heavy cream (cold)
- 1 tsp salt
- 5 tbsp ice-cold water

Directions:

1. Add the heavy cream to a food processor or stand mixer. Whip until the cream separates. After approximately 2-2½ minutes you will see it begin to thicken but continue whipping. After approximately 4 minutes, it should be entirely separated, and you will see buttery yellow solids and a cloudy liquid (buttermilk).

2. Once separated, pour in the water, this will help to separate the butter from the buttermilk.

3. Place a mesh sieve over a mixing bowl and pour the mixture into the sieve. The remaining liquid is the buttermilk.

4. Using clean hands, squeeze the butter solids to ensure that you have all the buttermilk possible. If you don't remove the buttermilk, your butter will be wet.

5. Season with salt to taste, transfer to a resealable glass jar, and store in the refrigerator for up to 6 weeks.

Blackberry and Honey Butter

This sweet and fruity berry butter will take your breakfast treats to the next level as it's ideal for slathering over warm waffles, pancakes, and French toast.

Servings: 24

Total Time: 5mins

Ingredients:

- 1 cup unsalted butter (at room temperature)
- 1 tbsp honey
- 2 tbsp confectioner's sugar
- 1 cup fresh blackberries

Directions:

1. Using an electric mixer, beat the butter until fluffy.
2. Add the confectioner's sugar and honey to the butter and beat again until smooth.
3. Add the blackberries, mix for 4-5 minutes until the berries have broken, and the butter is smooth.
4. Keep chilled for up to 14 days.

Blue Cheese Butter

Blue cheese butter makes a good steak, great!

Servings: 8

Total Time: 2hours 10mins

Ingredients:

- ½ cup butter (room temperature)
- 4 ounces blue cheese (room temperature)
- Small handful fresh parsley (finely chopped)

Directions:

1. Combine the butter with the blue cheese and parsley in a mixing bowl and with a metal fork, mash until incorporated.

2. Spoon the mixture onto a sheet of kitchen wrap and roll up into a log.

3. Chill in the fridge for a minimum of 2 hours before serving.

Butter Brandy Sauce

The boozy brandy butter sauce is a decadent topping for all sorts of desserts. Go on, spoil yourself!

Servings: 1-2

Total Time: 1hour 30mins

Ingredients:

- ¼ cup butter
- 1 cup icing sugar
- 2 tbsp brandy

Directions:

- In a bowl, cream the butter with the icing sugar until creamy light.
- Beat in the brandy.
- Transfer to the fridge to chill.
- Serve and enjoy.

California Olive and Rosemary Butter

Spread this savory butter on oven-baked Italian focaccia for a tasty appetizer that is easy to make.

Servings: 8

Total Time: 4mins

Ingredients:

- ½ cup butter (softened)
- 1 tbsp Californian ripe olives (pitted, minced)
- 2 tbsp fresh rosemary (minced)

Directions:

1. Add the softened butter to a bowl.
2. Stir the olives along with the minced rosemary into the butter to combine.
3. Transfer to the fridge to chill.
4. Use as needed.

Chocolate Butter

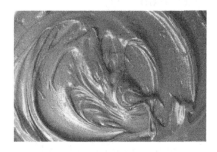

Rich and creamy, this chocolate butter is a tasty treat to spread over warm croissants or thick-cut toast.

Servings: 4

Total Time: 5mins

Ingredients:

- ½ cup unsalted butter (at room temperature)
- 1 tbsp cocoa powder
- ½ cup semi-sweet choc chips (melted)
- Pinch salt

Directions:

1. Using an electric mixer, beat the butter, cocoa powder, melted chocolate, and pinch of salt together for 60 seconds until smooth and silky.
2. Serve the butter at room temperature.

Maple and Parsley Butter

Sweet maple and grassy parsley make this the perfect butter to serve over meaty fish such as salmon.

Servings: 4

Total Time: 5mins

Ingredients:

- ½ cup salted butter (at room temperature)
- 2 tbsp maple syrup
- 1 tsp fresh parsley (minced)
- Pinch black pepper

Directions:

1. Using an electric mixer, beat together the salted butter, maple syrup, fresh minced parsley, and black pepper until fluffy and combined.
2. Keep chilled until ready to use.

Old-Fashioned Peach Butter

Fruit butter is less sweet than preserves or jam and a lot smoother too. You can spread it on English muffins, toast, pancakes or sandwiches. It also makes a spreadable filling for cakes or pies.

Servings: 4 (18 ounce) jars

Total Time: 10hours 10mins

Ingredients:

- 5½ pounds fresh peaches (pitted and chopped)
- 2½ cups sugar
- 4½tsp freshly squeezed lemon juice
- 1½ tsp ground cinnamon
- ¾ tsp ground cloves
- ½ cup quick-cooking tapioca

Directions:

1. In a mixing bowl, combine the chopped peaches with the sugar, fresh lemon juice, cinnamon, and cloves.

2. Transfer the mixture to a slow cooker of 5-quart capacity. Cover and on low, while occasionally stirring, cook for 8-10 hours until the fruit is very soft.

3. Stir in the tapioca and uncovered, cook on high for 60 minutes, or until thickened.

4. Transfer the butter into glass resealable jars and cool for 60 minutes, to room temperature.

5. Store in the fridge for up to 21 days.

6. Use as needed.

Red Wine Butter

This decadent red wine butter is just perfect for serving on top of a big juicy steak.

Servings: 8

Total Time: 3hours 15mins

Ingredients:

- ½ cup red wine
- 1 shallot (finely chopped)
- 1 cup salted butter (at room temperature)
- Small bunch fresh parsley (chopped)
- Salt and black pepper

Directions:

1. Add the red wine and shallot to a pan and place over moderately high heat. Bring to a boil and reduce down until the wine is almost gone. Take off the heat and allow to cool.

2. Add the butter, parsley, and red wine mixture to a bowl and beat until combined - season to taste with salt and black pepper.

3. Form the mixture into a log and wrap tightly in plastic wrap. Chill until the butter is solid enough to slice.

Slow-Cooked Apple Butter

This sweet and spicy, slow-cooked apple butter makes a lovely hostess gift.

Servings: 12-16

Total Time: 12hours 30mins

Ingredients:

- 6½ pounds apples (cored, peeled, and sliced)
- 1 cup brown sugar
- 1 cup granulated sugar
- ½ tsp nutmeg (freshly grated)
- 1 tbsp cinnamon
- ¼ tsp ground cloves
- ¼ tsp salt
- 1 tbsp vanilla essence

Directions:

1. Add the apple to a slow cooker.
2. In a small bowl, combine the brown sugar, granulated sugar, nutmeg, cinnamon, cloves, and salt. Scatter the mixture over the apple in the slow cooker.
3. Cook the mixture for 10 hours on low heat, remembering to stir occasionally until the mixture has a dark brown color and a thick texture.
4. At this point, stir in the vanilla essence and cook without the lid for another 2 hours.
5. Transfer the butter to a food processor and blitz to a smooth puree.
6. Keep the apple butter chilled for up to 14 days until ready serve.

Spicy Harissa Butter

Add spice to seafood or add flavor to chicken with this fiery North-African inspired butter.

Serving: 4-6

Total Time: 1hour 15mins

Ingredients:

- 1 pound unsalted butter (softened)
- 3 tbsp harissa
- 1 tbsp garlic (peeled, chopped)
- 2 tsp mint (chopped)
- ¼ tsp cumin
- ¼ tsp salt
- ⅛ tsp black pepper

Directions:

1. Add the butter, harissa, garlic, mint, cumin, salt, and black pepper to a bowl.
2. Using a rubber spatula fold and work the mixture to combine fully.
3. Divide the butter into two portions. Place each portion on a sheet of parchment paper and roll into a tube shape, twisting each end.
4. Transfer to the fridge for 60 minutes, until firm and chilled.
5. Use as required.

Three-Cheese Shallot Spread

This buttery center-piece is ideal for your next get-together and is a tasty treat to serve with crackers and red wine.

Servings: 12-16

Total Time: 3hours 40mins

Ingredients:

Shallots:

- 1 tbsp butter
- 2 large shallots (sliced)
- 1 tsp granulated sugar

Spread:

- ¼ cup butter (at room temperature)
- 8 ounces full-fat cream cheese (at room temperature)
- 1 cup Provolone cheese (shredded)
- 1 cup Cheddar cheese (shredded)
- 1 tsp Dijon mustard
- 2 tbsp fresh parsley (finely chopped)
- ¼ tsp salt
- ½ cup slivered almonds
- Crackers (to serve)

Directions:

1. First, prepare the shallots. Melt the butter in a skillet over moderate heat. Add the shallots and granulated sugar. Sauté for several minutes until brown and caramelized. Take off the heat and allow to cool for 10 minutes.

2. To an electric mixer bowl, add all the spread ingredients (butter, cream cheese, Provolone cheese, Cheddar cheese, Dijon mustard, parsley, and salt) and beat until fluffy and creamy.

3. Cover the butter with plastic wrap and chill for an hour.

4. Shape the chilled butter into a pine cone shape. Transfer to a serving plate. Insert the slivered almonds into the butter in rows to resemble a pine cone.

5. Chill for another couple of hours before serving with crackers.

Tomato Butter

You can spread this tasty tomato butter cold on crackers, add to grilled fish, steak or chicken, so it melts over the top or spread warm on muffins, and biscuits.

Servings: 6

Total Time: 5mins

Ingredients:

- 1 medium-size onion (peeled, finely chopped)
- 1 garlic clove (peeled, finely chopped)
- 8½ ounces butter
- 7 tbsp tomato paste
- 1½ tbsp freshly squeezed lemon juice
- 2 tsp salt
- 1 tsp black pepper
- 1 tsp paprika

Directions:

1. Add the onion and garlic to a bowl.
2. Add the butter, tomato paste, fresh lemon juice, salt, black pepper and paprika, and mash well with a metal fork.
3. Transfer to a serving bowl and enjoy.

Sauces

Anchovy Butter Sauce

This salty sauce perfectly complements all sorts of seafood dishes, grilled steak, and sautéed vegetables.

Servings: 4-6

Total Time: 12mins

Ingredients:

- 4 tbsp butter
- 1 (3 ounce) can anchovies
- ½ cup white wine
- 1 tbsp garlic (peeled, minced)
- 2 tbsp capers
- Dash of black pepper
- 1 lemon (thinly sliced, seeded)
- 1 tbsp fresh parsley (finely chopped)
- Paprika (to garnish)

Directions:

1. In a saucepan, heat to moderate-high heat and melt the butter.
2. Stir in the anchovies and with a fork, mash as they cook for 2 minutes.
3. Pour in the wine, and add the garlic, capers, a dash of black pepper, and 1 slice of lemon and slightly squeeze.
4. Cook for an additional 2-3 minutes and remove the pan from the heat.
5. Stir in the chopped parsley and remove and discard the slice of lemon.
6. Serve the sauce with seafood and garnish with the remaining lemon slices and a pinch of paprika.

Browned Butter Salted Caramel Sauce

Browned butter will give this salted caramel sauce a deliciously intense flavor. You can use it to top cheesecake, drizzle it over ice cream, serve it over apple pie or use it as a dipping sauce for fresh fruit.

Servings: 6-8

Total Time: 20mins

Ingredients:

- 6 tbsp butter
- 1 cup granulated sugar
- ½ cup + 2-3 tbsp heavy cream
- ¼ tsp sea salt

Directions:

1. Over moderate-low heat, add the butter to a small pan and cook until the butter melts and foams. Once the foam begins to disappear frequently swirl the pan.
2. Once the brown flecks or butter solids start to form at the bottom of the pan and are golden and fragrant (not brown), remove the pan from the heat.
3. Transfer the browned butter to a small bowl and put aside to cool.
4. Wash and dry the pan and add the sugar.
5. Over moderate heat, heat while stirring with a rubber spatula.

6. After 6-8 minutes, the sugar will begin to melt into the brown liquid and appear clumpy. As more clumps appear, they will begin to melt into the liquid.

7. When all of the sugar has dissolved into the liquid, whisk in the browned butter.

8. Reduce the heat to low and add the heavy cream while continually whisking. The mixture will bubble up and foam but continue to whisk. You may need to remove the pan from the heat to reduce the bubbling and create a glossy sauce.

9. Simmer on moderate-low heat, for 1-3 minutes, while frequently whisking.

10. Allow the sauce to cool and thicken.

11. Stir in the salt and serve.

Butter Sauce

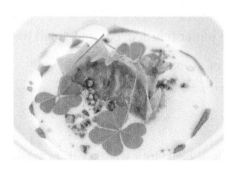

Serve this simple yet indulgent butter sauce with clams or lobsters.

Servings: 8

Total Time: 6mins

Ingredients:

- 1 tbsp freshly squeezed lemon juice
- 6 tbsp butter (chilled, cut into small pieces)
- Dash of ground red pepper

Directions:

1. Over low heat, in a small pan, heat the fresh lemon juice.
2. A little at a time, add the butter while constantly stirring with a whisk until the butter melts and is blended.
3. Stir in the red pepper and serve.

Cajun Butter Sauce

Serve this sauce as a decadent dip for steamed crab and transform a simple seafood dish into a sensational one!

Servings: 6

Total Time: 6mins

Ingredients:

- 8 tbsp butter (melted)
- 3 tbsp Old Bay seasoning
- 1 tbsp garlic powder
- 1 tsp cayenne pepper
- 1 tsp white pepper

Directions:

1. In a bowl, combine the melted butter with the Old Bay seasoning, garlic powder, cayenne, and white pepper. Stir until entirely blended.
2. Serve and enjoy.

Corn Butter Sauce

Hot sauce and lime juice cut through this sweet and creamy corn butter sauce.

Servings: 4-6

Total Time: 45mins

Ingredients:

- 5 fresh corn ears
- ⅓ cup water
- ¼ tsp sugar
- ¼ tsp kosher salt
- ¼ cup heavy cream
- 1 fresh bay leaf
- 2 sprigs fresh thyme
- ½ pound butter (diced)
- Hot sauce (to taste)
- Freshly squeezed lime juice (to taste)
- White truffle oil (to taste)

Directions:

1. To prepare the corn: First, husk the ears. Take a sharp knife and stand each ear on its end and slice downwards to remove the corn kernels from the cob.

2. Add the kernels to a food blender.

3. Take the knife in your right or left hand (depending on which is your dominant hand) and hold the corn cob core in the other. Using the blunt side of the knife, press it into the cob and beginning at the top near your hand, slide the length of the stalk downwards. Catch the corn juice in a bowl.

4. Repeat the process until all of the cores are scraped. Discard the cores and transfer the corn liquid to the food blender along with the cut kernels.

5. Pour in the water and add the sugar and salt to the food blender containing the corn kernels and corn liquid and puree until silky smooth.

6. Strain the mixture through a fine-mesh sieve into a stainless steel pan. Pour in the heavy cream and add the fresh bay leaf and sprigs of fresh thyme.

7. Place the pan over a moderate flame and increase the heat slowly until the mixture comes to boil while occasionally whisking. The corn starches will thicken the mixture.

8. Once the mixture has come to boil, remove from the heat.

9. Remove and discard the bay leaf and sprigs of thyme. Whisk in the diced butter. You may need to add a drop of water to adjust the consistency of the sauce. It also may need to be strained to remove any lumps.

10. Season with salt, 2-3 drops of hot sauce, fresh lime juice, and a drizzle of white truffle oil.

11. Serve the sauce, hot.

Cook's Note: Once cooled, the sauce can be stored in the refrigerator for up to 5 days.

Garlic Butter Sauce

Garlic butter sauce is a classic! Serve it for dipping lobster or crab legs or toss it with fettuccine to create a perfect pasta dish.

Servings: 4

Total Time: 8mins

Ingredients:

- ½ cup unsalted butter (room temperature)
- 4 garlic cloves (peeled, minced)
- ¼ cup fresh parsley or chives
- 1 tsp kosher salt

Directions:

1. In a bowl, combine the butter with the garlic, parsley and kosher salt and mix until entirely combined.
2. Transfer to an airtight container and store in the fridge for up to 7 days or until needed.
3. To use: Over moderate heat in a large frying pan, melt the garlic butter. Once the butter is fragrant, cook for 60 seconds before serving.

Lemon-Garlic and Sherry Butter Sauce

This sauce is all about the butter, and it's why it tastes as good as it does.   Toss it with pasta or serve it with fish; the choice is yours.

Servings: 6-8

Total Time: 20mins

Ingredients:

- ½ cup dry sherry
- ½ cup clam juice
- ½ cup whole milk
- 1 tbsp garlic (peeled, minced)
- 1 tbsp shallots (minced)
- 1 bay leaf
- 1 tbsp unsalted butter
- 1 tbsp all-purpose flour
- ½ pound unsalted butter
- 1 tbsp freshly squeezed lemon juice
- ½ tsp salt
- ½ tsp white pepper

Directions:

1. Add the dry sherry along with the clam juice, milk, garlic, shallots, and bay leaf to a small pan.

2. Over moderate heat, heat, and simmer until the liquid reduced by approximately half.

3. In a second pan of 1-quart capacity or more, prepare the roux: Over moderate heat, in a pan, heat 1 tablespoon of butter until foamy.

4. Scatter in the all-purpose flour, and with a metal whisk, whisk until combined and the roux is a tan color, for 2 minutes.

5. Slowly add the reduced clam juice mixture to the roux, quickly stirring to combine. At first, the mixture will bubble, but carry on adding the mixture while whisking to fully incorporate.

6. Reduce to low heat. Remove and discard the bay leaf.

7. Next, 2 tablespoons at a time, slowly whisk in the butter, allowing it to melt entirely between each additional.

8. Stir in the fresh lemon juice and season with salt and pepper. Add more clam stock or water to thin out the consistency, if needed.

9. Serve.

Mustard Butter Sauce

Add a creamy sauce to grilled fish and meats with this rich mustard sauce. It is especially good with steak and green beans.

Servings: 4

Total Time: 20mins

Ingredients:

- 1 tsp white wine vinegar
- 2 tsp white wine
- 2 shallots (peeled, very thinly chopped)
- 1 tsp heavy cream
- 3½ ounces unsalted butter (chilled, diced)
- Salt and freshly ground black pepper
- 1 tbsp wholegrain mustard

Directions:

1. In a small pan, combine the white wine vinegar with the white wine and shallots and cook over moderate heat until the mixture has reduced to a syrup consistency.
2. Stir in the heavy cream and cook to reduce a bit more.
3. Add the butter, whisking until it is amalgamated - taste and season with salt and pepper.
4. Stir in the mustard and pass through a fine-mesh sieve.
5. Serve immediately.

Orange Butter Sauce

This creamy, tangy sauce works extremely well with mild-tasting fish, including haddock and trout, as well as scallops, lobster, and crab.

Servings: 2-4

Total Tie: 25mins

Ingredients:

- Freshly squeezed juice of 2 oranges
- 2 tsp orange zest
- ½ cup white wine
- 2 tsp shallots (minced)
- ½ pound unsalted butter
- Salt and white pepper

Directions:

1. Add the orange juice, orange zest, white wine, and shallots to a pan over a moderate-high heat and cook until the consistency of syrup and significantly reduced.
2. On low heat, 1 tablespoon at a time, vigorously and continually whisk in the butter. You will need to add it slowly to create a silky smooth texture. Do not allow the sauce to boil.
3. Season with salt and white pepper to taste.

Peanut Butter Sauce

This versatile sauce is as good with Asian noodles as it is as a party dip.

Servings: 6-8

Total Time: 10mins

Ingredients:

- ¾ cup creamy peanut butter
- ¼ cup rice vinegar
- ⅓ cup reduced-sodium soy sauce
- 3 tbsp honey
- ½ tsp ground ginger
- 1-2 medium cloves garlic (peeled, minced)
- ¼ tsp red pepper flakes
- 2-4 tbsp coconut milk
- 4 tbsp water (if needed)
- Roasted peanuts (chopped, to serve, optional)
- Red pepper flakes (to garnish)

Directions:

1. In a mixing bowl, whisk the peanut butter with the rice vinegar, soy sauce, honey, ground ginger, garlic, red pepper flakes, and coconut milk until entirely combined. You may need to add water to thin out the consistency.

2. Either serve as a sauce or if using as a dip, transfer to a bowl and garnish with chopped peanuts and red pepper flakes.

Sage and Brown Butter Sauce

Add pizza to poultry, pasta, mash potatoes, and more with this aromatic sauce.

Servings: 4-6

Total Time: 8mins

Ingredients:

- 8 tbsp butter
- 1 garlic cloves (peeled, crushed and chopped)
- ¼ cup fresh sage leaves (coarsely chopped)
- ⅛ tsp freshly ground black pepper

Directions:

1. In a pan over low to moderate heat, melt the butter. As soon as the butter begins to bubble slightly, add the chopped garlic.
2. Stir the garlic into the butter for 60 seconds before adding the sage and continue stirring while cooking for an additional 1-2 minutes. The butter should be a very light brown color with a nutty, rich aroma.
3. Season with black pepper and serve.

Tabasco Butter Sauce

Transform crab cakes with this Tabasco and butter sauce. It's ready from pan to plate in no time at all and can elevate all sorts of dishes with red, peppery and hot flavor.

Servings: 4

Total Time: 15mins

Ingredients:

- 1 tbsp canola oil
- 2 shallots (finely chopped)
- ¼ cup celery (finely chopped)
- ½ red bell pepper (seeded, stemmed and finely chopped)
- 3 cloves of garlic (peeled, finely chopped)
- 1 tbsp parsley stems (finely chopped)
- 3 sprigs of fresh thyme
- 1 tsp whole black peppercorns
- 2-3 whole chile de árbol
- ¼ cup white wine vinegar
- 2 tbsp white wine
- 2 tbsp Tabasco sauce
- ½ cup heavy cream
- 6 tbsp unsalted butter (cut into 1" squares)
- Fresh lemon juice (to taste)
- Salt (to taste)

Directions:

1. Over moderate heat, heat the oil in a pan.
2. Add the shallots followed by the celery, bell pepper, and garlic and sauté for 2 minutes, until softened but not brown.
3. Next, add the parsley, thyme, black peppercorns, and chile de arbol. Sauté for 60 seconds before deglazing the pan with vinegar and wine. Reduce the liquid until almost dry.
4. Add the Tabasco sauce, to taste, and pour in the heavy cream.
5. Bring the mixture to boil and cook for approximately 2 minutes, until the cream is thickened.
6. Remove the sauce from the heat and one piece at a time, whisk the butter into the sauce.
7. Strain the sauce through a fine-mesh sieve and season with fresh lemon juice and salt.
8. Serve warm.

Author's Afterthoughts

I would like to express my deepest thanks to you, the reader, for making this investment in one my books. I cherish the thought of bringing the love of cooking into your home.

With so much choice out there, I am grateful you decided to Purch this book and read it from beginning to end.

Please let me know by submitting an Amazon review if you enjoyed this book and found it contained valuable information to help you in your culinary endeavors. Please take a few minutes to express your opinion freely and honestly. This will help others make an informed decision on purchasing and provide me with valuable feedback.

Thank you for taking the time to review!

Christina Tosch

About the Author

Christina Tosch is a successful chef and renowned cookbook author from Long Grove, Illinois. She majored in Liberal Arts at Trinity International University and decided to pursue her passion of cooking when she applied to the world renowned Le Cordon Bleu culinary school in Paris, France. The school was lucky to recognize the immense talent of this chef and she excelled in her courses, particularly Haute Cuisine. This skill was recognized and rewarded by several highly regarded Chicago restaurants, where she was offered the prestigious position of head chef.

Christina and her family live in a spacious home in the Chicago area and she loves to grow her own vegetables and herbs in the garden she lovingly cultivates on her sprawling estate. Her and her husband have two beautiful children, 3 cats, 2 dogs and a parakeet they call Jasper. When Christina is not hard at work creating beautiful meals for Chicago's elite, she is hard at work writing engaging e-books of which she has sold over 1500.

Make sure to keep an eye out for her latest books that offer helpful tips, clear instructions and witty anecdotes that will bring a smile to your face as you read!

Made in the USA
Las Vegas, NV
15 October 2024

96927772R00062